ZEBRA LASHES

Rikki Santer

Fernwood
PRESS

Zebra Lashes

©2024 Rikki Santer

Fernwood Press
Newberg, Oregon
www.fernwoodpress.com

All rights reserved. No part may be reproduced
for any commercial purpose by any method without
permission in writing from the copyright holder.

Printed in the United States of America

Cover photo: Sandra Feen

ISBN 978-1-59498-137-1

for Marc and Parker,
sweet scallywags I adore

Also by Rikki Santer:

Front Nine: A Biography of Place
Clothesline Logic
Fishing for Rabbits
Kahiki Redux
Make Me That Happy
Dodge, Tuck, Roll
In Pearl Broth
Drop Jaw
Head to Toe of It
How to Board a Moving Ship
Stopover
Resurrection Letter: Leonora, Her Tarot, and Me

Contents

Also by Rikki Santer: 4
FROM THE GECKO 11
   Zebra Lashes 12
   House of Bears 13
   Bat Faith 15
   Eel Love 17
   Sijo At Dusk 19
   Chicken Envy 20
   Life Poodle 21
   Eco Dysphagia 22
   Thought, Song, ... 23
FOOL HEARTY 25
   If You Have to Ask 26
   Some Things I Encountered
      While Conversing 27
   Food for Thought at Philosophy Hall 29
   Manifesto for My Pockets 30
   Score for Teapot Duet 31

Sleep Study 32
Postcard From Elsewhere 34
Morning Collage 35
Does Cloud Make You Think of Data or Sky? 36

FURLED BROW 37
Knots: A Ledger 38
On Candy Lane 39
City Pool Swimming Lesson 41
Evergreen 43
When Auntie Kissed a Beat, ... 44
Shopping Center Tipsy 46
Some Fun Facts about Berries 48
Dining with Parents 49
Attic 50
This Autumn My Son 51
Leavings 52
Missed the Weather Report 53
Trace Decay 54
Sock 56
When Green Changes Its Mind 57
Blood-Dark 58

WITH BAITED BREATH 61
What I Learned from Ambrose Bierce 62
Destiny News 64
All the Days of Forgetting 66
Midnight at the Mill 67
The Haserot Angel Holds Court 68
Row, Row, Row Your Exquisite Boat 69
Husk 70
Stepsisters at Large 71
Dolly Parton, a Theory of 73
Chef-O-Nette 74

Freeway Ramp 75
Dietrich 76
Kindred Reckoning 78
What Belongs to the Moment 80
How to Outwit Oblivion 81
Resurrection Letter: Leonora,
   Her Tarot, and Me (in seventeen parts) 82

END TRAILS 99
Hand Shadows 100
Release Recurring 102
Blood 104
Golden Shovel: She Just Packed up
   Her Stuff and Left* 105
Box Like No Other 106
The Alchemy of View 107
Some Security Questions 108
Ode to the Candidate Commercials
   of Ohio's Special 15th Congressional Seat
   Election August 2021 109
Yard Signs for the Apocalypse 110
Tipping Points 111
The Expectation of More
   (A Golden Shovel after Shakespeare) 113
What's Left on the Plate 114

In Gratitude 115
Acknowledgments 117
Title Index 121
First Line Index 125

"I asked the Zebra, are you black with white stripes? Or white with black stripes? And the zebra asked me, Are you good with bad habits? Or are you bad with good habits? Are you noisy with quiet times? Or are you quiet with noisy times? Are you happy with some sad days? Or are you sad with some happy days? Are you neat with some sloppy ways? Or are you sloppy with some neat ways? And on and on and on and on and on and on he went. I'll never ask a zebra about stripes...again."
—Shel Silverstein

"I saw its story through through the brush of my eyelashes."
—Madeline Gins

"The zebras were grazing on the African svelte."
—Deep gratitude
to Daniel Menaker, author of
*The African Svelte:
Ingenious Misspellings That Make Surprising Sense*
for inspiring my section headings.

FROM THE GECKO

Zebra Lashes

Father liked to warn me about
the black and white of things
and how prayer can only be expected

to leave behind a trail for tumbling
into a rabbit hole. Make sure nothing
is too realistic he'd say and when in doubt,

lean into the language of bray and bark.
And don't trust the curve of the earth
or eyelashes on creatures that have them,

for the stye of prequel is misleading at best
because what will be extinct, will be extinct.
But not today I say when the young woman

at her first-day, minimum-minimum-wage
job with her purple fingernails too long
for the keyboard and her plastic

eyelashes too heavy for a smile was
trying damned hard which should
amount to something like zoo cages

that want us to be in saving states
of mind as when my small son and I
lingered to watch a young Grevy's zebra

that was taking a shit while she batted
her eyelashes like a sugar baby,
snout low and gaze recused.

House of Bears

after photographs by Dmitry Kokh

From a camera drone, the running
buzz of tiny propellers draws
them out from weary windows
and busted-out door frames of

a long-abandoned weather station
on Kolyuchin Island in the Chukchi Sea.
This fabular nest for polar bears
looks like an eerie movie set

with its rickety front porch
and weathered walls.
Raisin eyes and plush-toy snouts
pose for the logic of their curiosity

and the showy illusion
of their translucent fur.
I imagine *ACTION!*
and then it's the scraping

of claws over warped floorboards,
shortwave static from phantom
radio channels, ghosts of brewed
coffee and boisterous laughter.

Do these Arctic creatures take turns gnawing
on a forgotten broomstick to clean their
incisors, lumber to corners of the house as
it teeters from side to side, rumble around

empty oil barrels in the yard so
the ventricles of their hearts fill
with joy? I linger on these photos
through the night, my gaze longing

as their dark eyes gaze back. A milky
sun rises on an overcast morning
as the bears wander through
this deserted building on a rocky shore.

They will hunt, swim among the ice
floes, survive stormy winds and rain
and the fog that will push up against
their warm haunches, until it doesn't.

Bat Faith

We're not upside down—
you're upside down
the bats reminded me
from their bat house
in my neighbor's yard.
So don't see us, they
warned, like folded up
umbrellas because one
more cliche will deflate
us all. But we do dangle
like Yahweh and in
haywire flight we flit
into and out of your mirrors.
With rainbow as backdrop,
our colony streams into dusk
from sandy caves of your
darkest nightmares
for we clean our babies'
faces just like you, and
when the occasion offers,
hibernate in wine coolers.
We hear the idea
of everything, cling
longer than you can,
and leave commas
in the air with fine
fabric of our wings.

So on my back
deck that night when
a single bat soared low
again and again just over
my head in turnings
that led into
deeper turnings—
instead of feeling
fear of entanglement,
I felt abiding joy as when
the gait of angels is near.

Eel Love

You bring
        your tabernacle
                down low
almost graze
        my hair

then let out
        the eels
                that braid
out from
        your mouth.

On parchment
        your plan sends
                me palpitations—

Eel Love,
        coil caresses
                my throat.
You are the
        sea within

the sea, I am
        cameo
                appearance
as salty
        stream.

So many
  willow leaves,
     the parentheses
that embed
   your lore:

eel slime,
  patina of
     imperial
wound,
     umbilical
entrance,
  then writhing
voyage of
    too-muchness
    not-enoughness,

murky ballet
  of approach
    and avoidance.
Terrible
   certainty

terrible
  pendulum—
    the Eel
Question
   swims
with me,
  keeps me
    alive.

Sijo at Dusk

Noble buck at corn feeder. Broken antler, back leg dangling.
Gentle doe at his side, licking blood wounds, nuzzling
 bent snout.
Backyard ravine's tale of life. May loved ones be near me
 when I die.

Chicken Envy

You are a walking flower
      pecking away
           in my neighbor's backyard.
With your thin-lipped grin
      you say things to me in chicken.
              You might as well
    be queen of something
        so I imagine your tiny high heels
                and tiara of golden kernels.
You give me thicker yokes
      than Kroger's   and most nights I dream
        of cooing   *My Sweet Girl*
      as you nap
           in my lap.
    Remnants from
             Chick-fil-A or Colonel Sanders
    no longer in my trash can
        and Henny Pennys muted
    in my Twitter feed.
How mild your terraced life
    your reliable rhythms of emptyfull.
        Your chickless eggs sustenance
for my fruitless ovaries of sorrow.

Life Poodle

> after Alan Shapiro

Lifeblood of curlicues, shlup shlup of tongue and snout that welcomes the morning sun. Sometimes tethered, sometimes vying for dog park hierarchy and its standard, miniature, toy of free range. And when you can't find what you're looking for, use your nose or gnaw what's good for gnawing. Know the trot of best-in-show distracts as does each bowl of sautéed steak. Scissorhands can groom any bitch or stud for tufts and rosettes of circus play and each echo of bark, arf, or yelp reminds that you're still here and that there's no other stink that stinks quite like you. Remember to run from the newspaper but lavish laps that promise comfort and glee. And when you snarl and want to go for the throat, instead lift your leg or squat then whack back and forth your compliant tail to the singsong melodies of *good dog.*

Eco Dysphagia

    after Sophie Knee's sculpture, *I Can't Swallow*

Your swallow bird corpse
served up elegant
on a chinoiserie plate—
our porcelained detachment
stuck in our throats.
T.S. Eliot lamented in Latin
When will I be like the swallow
so that I can stop being silent?
Another spring and we ignore
your arabesque spiraling
in open skies closing up
with wind turbines or peppered
less and less with the aerial
plankton that you crave.
Did your forked tail house
an army of avian lice?
Was your salt marsh nest
devoured by ocean flooding?
Did you spend last days
rolling your head for
hot breezes to comb
your parched neck?

Thought, Song,

particle, wave, the glorious inhale/
exhale of it. Two cardinals dither
daily at our address.
My wry husband believes that drones
will be our next state bird
but I believe in you—our backyard familiars,
priestly robes of Ohio, red beyond
any of our reds.

Beneath the ceiling of your soaring,
you've stayed put in our ravine, life mates
under a biblical edge of sky.
Together, you are the opening lines
of our mornings, schooling us in harmony,
our vowels between your vowels.

You are the sum of our location
decorating our spring dogwood,
a clear-windowed nest filled
with quivering guillemets
for whom you share their feeding
with unspoken fairness.

You both light on our deck's railing, leap
onto your breakfast table, porcelain plate
filled with blueberries and black-oil
seeds and sometimes, in my
aptitude for stillness,
mother pecks from my palm.
I think you come close because
you can escape so easily.

This winter, swish of scarlet frosting,
black masks that seem to wait for our notice.
Children hum in the next room.
Husband brings me a hot toddy.
Kiss between us, our tongues mealworms
twirling for sustenance.
Where we've been doesn't matter.
Where we fit so perfectly
grows wings.

FOOL HEARTY

If You Have to Ask

If you have to ask twice what's under the hood, you already know the sky is heading your way with mammary clouds for your soliloquy. If you have to keep asking, *what's next?* then you just found in your back pocket three lyrical bulletins of hemming and hawing that survived the wash cycle. If you have to ask for another paper cup of watered-down lemonade from twin nieces who enterprise like their stockbroker daddy, then you are betwixt and between a Freudian tale. If every time you ask if this next haircut could be kinder, you're still not ready to meet absolution of fraying self-image or deep disappointment in over-priced, goji-berry smoothies.
If you have to ask if a podcast can be the fount of enlightenment, you need to open your eyes immediately and pay attention to oncoming traffic. If you have to ask if a butterfly net would be an appropriate accessory for singles-bar-weekends, you must know that hovering braggarts get stuck in mesh, too. If you have to ask if you could swallow that dazzling explosion of your son's unbridled laughter, you know that soon you will be gnawing on its still life. When they ask you if you'd be okay if a snail follows you for the rest of your life, you know you've guzzled too much spirit serum, and now it just doesn't matter.

Some Things I Encountered While Conversing

1
Thought balloons
can sparkle.

2
Silence
may masquerade
as effective
one-liners.

3
Everything he said
had an asterisk
after it.

4
Phlegm refrains
more fluid
with bourbon.

5
A shush
is a shush
is a shush.

6
When I tried
to reason with him,
spiders flew
from his mouth.

7
Videoconferencing
with myself
still requires
high angles.

8
Magic 8 Balls
and Ouija planchettes
pretend to care.

9
Semi-colons
evaporate faster
than ghosts.

10
Hiccups became
my savior
from tedium.

11
Her purring
adhered me
to the moon.

12
His penumbra
wrapped around me
like a boa.

13
I ended up
torturing the point
with precision.

14
At Porky's
my intoxicated secrets
were squandered
in pig latin.

Food for Thought at Philosophy Hall

It was a brisk, fall evening on campus when I had misread the time for the symposium *On Knowing* and got to the lecture a bit early. Having side-stepped dinner, I decided to look for a vending machine and found one in the dimly lit basement. Its bill acceptor was a bit sticky, but it took my crumpled dollar anyway, and I was relieved because I knew it would never take a same dollar twice. The glass case was smudged with handprints and grime which made it hard to decipher the offerings, but my stomach was growling so I tried A1 on the key pad. A tray rumbled, and then, inside the pick-up box sat a Rhode Island Red with her egg. Which one landed there first I could not decipher. I had no appetite for raw yoke, and frankly I was hoping for a Snickers, so I tried another dollar, this one crisp and maybe clean of any residue of paradox. But when I pressed B2, a can of Schrödinger's Ocean Fish Pâté for Kittens tumbled down the shute, and I promptly realized I wasn't *that* famished. One more dollar bill in my wallet, a last stab at probability. What outcome could a Z13 provide? Again grumbling from the machine's belly and then into its solemn dispenser an either/or sandwich with a bright packet of sweet and sour, after which I promptly made my way up to the top floor, just in time to take a seat in the balcony's last row where the rustling of cellophane was mine alone to hear.

Manifesto for My Pockets

after John M. Sokol

the this / the that / the these / a day
glow Post-it note origami / anagram
puzzle that could nag a ram / splinter
I will complain of / divining rod
toothpick that's ready to ponder /
a catseye too voluptuous for words /
three greasy pennies mumbling
inflation / thumb-sized ax for forging
stubborn ideas / stubby pencil with
teeth-marked messages / a matchbook
of indiscretion / creased maple leaf
brooding the past / the coil of moment /
eyelash of betrayal / teabag of regret /
lint wad of lost punchline / shard
of fortune-cookie fortune urging
me on / lucky planet of a pebble

Score for Teapot Duet

Meet a willing teapot.
With its Earl Grey sighs, allow it to flirt.
Dab its steam behind your ears.
Stroke its porcelain roundness with dreams of lacy red negligee.
Sip on your honeyed inhibitions.
Let teapot pour you another virgin cup of wonder.
Put on some ruby red lipstick
and press your hottie sultriness
onto its spout.

Sleep Study

One electrode would have been one too many but now I have a spider web of them all over my body for this polysomnogram which right off the bat is a term that causes me anxiety and I'm stiff under threadbare blankets beneath an infrared camera eye that seems accusatory already so I retaliate imagining that the technician in the other room is picking her nose and then wonder how the hell a bear-head sketch in the magazine on the nightstand could snatch eight million dollars if it weren't scrawled by the hand of da Vinci and the ceiling here ain't no Sistine Chapel but wait that was Michelangelo's doing not da Vinci's so the water stains keep me entertained for a while in a Rorschach kind of way until the leatherback sea turtle gets me worrying about the extinction of yet another species and now the plastic microphone taped to my neck feels like the hand of my last date who insisted on karaoke but I need to stay calm waiting for the Ambien in spite of the rubber tubing that sits in my nose and Patty—my technician whose name gives me some relief along with her ID tag of smiling bunnies—gets on the two-way radio to encourage me to relax which does just the opposite so the hours slink on as I turn and turn like a rotisserie chicken sometimes switching on the TV perched high into the wall like a hospital room fixture but the parade of infomercials for air fryers, exercise implements and advanced whitening formulas doesn't numb me and I wonder if the brocade curtains would be better off if a window was behind them and now I have a sickly sweet swill in my mouth from the framed Thomas Kinkade prints on every wall of this clinical bedroom and the greasy fingerprints someone left on the bedside lamp send me lusting for French fries so it's back to the skewer and Patty is getting frustrated that her velvety just-try-to-relaxes aren't working and she tries piping in ocean waves and sea gulls but that only makes me feel like I have to pee so at 4 a.m. she surrenders to my famine of REM and sends me home with my shoulders slumped, my satin pillow deflated and my pjs damp under my trench coat to wind my way through lonely streets to my front door where I climb the stairs to my Tempur-Pedic where the fragile bubbles of home remedy light down and I dream of floating over lapping shorelines and swimming with porpoises.

Postcard From Elsewhere

Here we are, a bedazzled crew of yahoos, careening in the last bus toward Planet 9, packed tight in this cosmic photo booth, with Ms. Frizzle at the helm spitting out fun facts as we all try to gin up some cartoonish enthusiasm for outgrowing our meridians in this dream nest, this house party in rogue orbit with dapper Colonel Mustard sequestered in the nerve center sorting recaps from prequels and Betty Boop shimmies in her market-driven algorithm while the dark matter between us contains all our primal screams and everything that will be and ever was.

Morning Collage

This poem passes through wheels of color
    little tom-toms of blues and reds and purples
        to fatten my hearing for the locomotive
            of my early morning mind
                that lets out plenty of kite string
so I can hover above the tracks
      that obsession delivers
              to recount the sleeves
  of the burgundy dress
                  I wore last night
        the smear of scarlet lipstick
    the cobalt of tongues,   and now
      the magenta spin of ticktock ache
              in *Swear-ta-god I'll call tomorrow.*

DOES CLOUD MAKE YOU THINK OF DATA OR SKY?

> Prada advertisement in *The New York Times Style Magazine*
> February 21, 2021

Every click, tap, and swipe turns
into restless bytes then seasoned
to taste by hungry harvesters—
transient moments measured
and mined. Strap me instead
to moonlight, catapult me
into a rumspringa among
night clouds lofty and
pinnacled, whorling like
spiral staircases—fleeting
breathwork in the sky.

FURLED BROW

Knots: A Ledger

One lasso for landing another one-night stand, tightening
    around one more next morning.
Two ends braided into an Arabian's lush mane emerging
    through the bedroom window.
Three twists that predate ax and wheel, ghosts of four hands
    that fashioned rope fossils.
Five bowlines for five drunk rabbits, coming out of five holes,
    circling five tipsy trees, then back again.
A clove hitch slipped for six renegades who entangle reasonable
    threads that could anchor the inevitable windstorm.
Seven paracords coil like question marks in hovering
    helicopters; eight lechers piloting, hungry for hearts.
Nine Gordian knots entwined with ten Gordian knots ignoring
    Lady Liberty weeping as they snake around her neck.
Eleven working-ends ready for binding as pearl gray
    skies metastasize after another election night.
A dozen macramé plant hangers on garage sale table—
    smirking neighbors taunting hippie-dinosaur
    readied for the fight.

On Candy Lane

My scribbled life
lines up—smudged
frames in photo booth
cartoons—me wearing
low hats, squinty eyes,
candy cigarettes between
my powdered-sugar lips.

There's no room
for ambush here.
I had it coming
rolling in honey.

Taffy dreams most nights
that stretch two and two
together, bon bons inside
bonbons that lead in,
lead out to sticky stick
men, women nougats,
souvenirs of sweet tooth
that has taken me this far.

I seem to only see them
when they see me. Sharp-edged
rock candy in the alleyways,
Red Hots under tongues
in constant motion,
parable of saccharine okays.

Still, constellations of lollipops
pull me, their swirls of
wild color. And the fairy floss
of cotton candy can send me
hovering into the faraway
milkiness of Milky Way.

City Pool Swimming Lesson

It was my Atlantic
and Pacific where
summer bodies
blossomed on its shore
or soared like albatrosses
down a slick, yellow slide
where concession
stand was messy
with salt and goo,
where the changing
rooms were graffiti,
chipped sea green,
and floor puddles
up to my ankles
      then my first violence
when clammy hands
of a teenaged instructor
hurled me into the deep
for instinct's floating
but instead my fingers
grasped murky walls
closing in
gravel nipping
at my toes
scraping my knees
eyes and lungs stinging
mouth flooding
      then my mother's face
and arms sputtering through,
lifting me to her warm breasts,
pounding heart, carrying

me back, swaddling me
tight in her embrace
as we trembled
together
on the edge
of a plastic chaise
my tiny tears doll
face down in the sand
      what a day feels like
when it never leaves
and where its drink
becomes blueprint for
for an aging nonswimmer.

Evergreen

I was raised by a Canadian hemlock, her perfume
smelled like freedom from pointy days.
I named her Homeland, my secret bunker beneath
her dense arms and mothering coolness.

I brought her gifts—Barbie heads and my favorite
yo-yo wedged into her pine needle duff.
I took home her gifts—pinecone soldiers, rosy
purple violets and mushrooms creamy white.

Trees were eternal then. In the grove across
the street—never just one birthed sweet
apples and together the whole family hosted
confetti parties for the honeybees. Today,

a new city, a much older life and the anxious
blur of bison tails fenced into the heat of a
metro park's prairie summer. Along the trail,
rising darkness is left to fewer crickets, fewer

fireflies, more plastic bottles, more cigarette
butts. Down the road Walnut Woods—woods
no longer, but sterile orchards of lampposts,
concrete, and hybrid grass turf.

In my front yard a Ponderosa pine planted
by another family now bends a tall obtuse
angle into the sky. My husband fears above
ground its thick roots will surrender to fierce

winds and massacre a neighbor's roof,
so he contemplates preemptive action
and I, after each twilight run, stroke
her sticky trunk for the sake of another day.

When Auntie Kissed a Beat,

urban stew swizzled her tongue,
pastrami on warm rye arrested

any of her afterthoughts
of Wonder bread dough balls

commandeered from crust.
His Luckies swiveled

between her fingers like
pipe dreams, so urbane,

so hip. Her thrift-store beret
dangled from the bedpost

while a shot, a toke, a snort
grew grammar in her mouth.

His kisses were swift and hard,
droplets of blood from her lips

were ellipses on napkins
of his poetry and for her

it was one subterranean,
nascent week, swaying

in lifestyle that bongoed
and bebopped her heart.

Then a crisp bus ticket,
dog-eared copy of *Howl*

left on her dresser, and a
story that grew plumper

each Thanksgiving until
a headstone put a period on it:

IF YOU CAN READ THIS,
YOU ARE STANDING ON
MY BOOBS, DIG?

Shopping Center Tipsy

Hey, Tequila Mockingbird, there's a sparrow's
nest in your sign's O and a line of rock pigeons
perched like a shortage of ideas, warming
their feet on the electrical wires that italicize
your parking lot. Over there a ragged
man in a motorized shopping cart
commandeered from Walmart
draws circles around the SUVs
that pose like elephants resting
on their haunches. And I am wondering
how many parading goslings
will it take to discourage
that purple-haired motorcyclist.
On the sidewalk in front of Nothing
Bundt Cakes a signature of chewed-up
bubble-gum wads declare F U C K U
which makes me chuckle because
I'm trying to stumble on
happiness that doesn't mind
liquored up pretense or woodpecker
persistence for every small enterprise
to feel like a muppet reboot
of Dante's Circle of Angels.
Yet maybe I shouldn't be in the mood
for projecting but I am

in the mood for another blunt
and hell no not a gummy
that sugars its intent
but a sequence
of long&deep&out
that reminds my lungs
that I'm still in charge.
So here I am crouching
on a concrete lip in front of
Sentimentality Is Us thumbing
Morse code messages onto
my key fob to remind the Fiat
that it won again in our parking
lot game of hide-and-seek
but wait
the honks from a V
of Canada geese heading for
a nursing home pond
where a plastic swan
has sunk into a murky bottom
remind me that's where
my mother waits for me—
now I'm late for lunch again
but this time
our last one together.

Some Fun Facts about Berries

I can't decide if my Honey is berry—
raz, straw, black, or blue.

Tiny hairs on his head are tender styles, leftovers
from when he blossomed, but safe for my lips.

Like ripe tomatoes in his favorite ketchup or his
guacamole's creamy avocados, he is fruit unmistakably true.

Yet he could also be berry aggregate with tiny seeds of
personality that sweeten the palate or sideswipe the tongue.

He likes to shoot off runners to multiply crop, like when a surprise
morning bouquet knows how to ground a thunderstorm at night.

Some say berries boost a brain's housekeeping mechanism, so
maybe his underwear drawer is a very berry aberration.

But for all his druplets and fuzzy calyx, I am grateful
for my Strawberry, luscious jam and jelly absolute.

Dining with Parents

We were sugar packet missiles
across the restaurant table
while waiting for our food

Mashed potato and pea volcanoes
Pompeii with our food

Lemon slices as eyewear
fashion with our food

Broccoli spears between cushions
camouflage with our food

Butter knife for ketchup chest stains
theater with our food

Boogers in the gravy
sibling rivalry with our food

Chocolate pudding in spoon catapults
spankings with our food.

Attic

The precinct of my night's mind
leads me to a hidden door
in the Airbnb Tudor that opens
to the vertical power
of heat, an empty holding
cell for abandonment.
Sprocket snoring swirls
from bedrooms below,
nudges these dirty crevices
as early eastern sun begins
its wake through a lone window
to shiver cobwebs, to swaddle
dust ghosts of chairs and trunks
and sled that once lived there.

Back home a package arrives
from a library's anonymous
donation box three states away.
I am recipient found in cyberspace
and I am grateful for the browning,
tattered pages of photo album reunion—
so many smiling poses, birthday
cakes, and tender embraces
of extended family long gone, along
with a scrawled Post-it note
on the opening sheet,
found in our attic.

This Autumn My Son

> *...as if hope and will could make magic...*
> Dana Levin

Your ginger beard
these slippery paths carpeted
with ginger leaves surrendered
hickory nut shells rattle behind your forehead
your boy in man lurks inside the brackets
alongside too many flavors of pain
your heart a sad fist with extension cord frayed
your isolation a throbbing hologram
won't Chance step in to offer you a compass
through the brambles, some flickering joy
a bit of moonlight on your tongue
a tenderness to graze you.

Leavings

Her wobbly handwriting in signature purple ink
on the face of a tiny envelope under perfumed hankies—
7 extra pearls for choker she had written.
A hidden survivor in the nursing home drawer
where the velvet box was stolen, now nacre of her leaving.

They wanted her belongings out before the funeral,
so in haste we harvested mostly chaff into paper
ream cartons—frayed sweaters, worn slippers, stash
of newspaper comic strips to be mailed to her minions.

But the irritant she regretted to leave behind,
this mother, high priestess of accessory, was memory
of her mourning that loss of pearl necklace by a faceless thief
whose face she probably saw each day after.

Pearl necklace, favorite gift from my father who left too early,
Chanel No. 5 that lingered on each lustrous bead
after so many cha cha nights they spent together
and her master plan—that a strand's legacy would continue
around the neck of her only daughter.

Seven orphaned pearls sucked from the shell
of maternal desire returned to their browning
envelope to nestle with sachet and folded tongues
of my scarves for a life still detached but tethered.

Missed the Weather Report

    My father saw surprises
whether good or bad—
        places to be on your toes.

        Late April snowfall cover,
a morning startle—
            pink tulip heads bow in prayer.

        Sunshine drifts across ravine,
all sugar-coated—
            cardinal wings reach through tall trees.

        Peanuts on the back deck chairs
like sundae toppings—
            five eager squirrels mining.

Snow mottles down from branches,
overstayed welcome—
        all hosta leaves salute noon,

                uncanny spring
                father gone.

Trace Decay

    My slippers shuffle me
                room to room. How to
rehearse memory—beanbag
  or cornhole, charlatan or cardsharp, facto-pivot
                          or cow-tipped, my gut
         tells me what to remember. I suspect
I'm secretly birthday cake backward
          for questions that tremble in the air,
    myths fatigued but willing. When walls
      arrive, all possibilities of skin and algorithm collude
  (puzzle of bygone tattoos). Braided membranes of lies
      and truths quiver into places where reality bends,
        (sudden face where no face should be).
        My story straddles
    the in-between. I prefer to call my venous lake
      Venus Lake
            or savor the rust of you
          and you. Raw yolk in my teeth, bower bird
        at my feet, honeyed
              sleep sour on my tongue.

    Recall
        the ashes that rest
on a peacock's tail
        from your self-congratulatory cigar,
    ancient scent of a moist and misty
            river source, draft growler
        whose fruit bomb
            is blueberry puree/grapefruit zest and not
        what Papa would recognize at all. Indeed,
    if I could I would, yet At is where I'm at,
        slightly tannic lies ahead—
maybe our chestnuts still roasting, your pickled herring
        sweating in a jar but always me
    teething on shards
            of gone and gone by.

Sock

Some say dryers eat us.
What will I do
without my other?
Neruda's were sharks, cannons.
Now I am a lonely damsel.
In murky water I fumbled
for a ledge. Snagged by a pier
of contrarian stones,
I'm caked with bitterness,
tortured by flies. The tide
is slopping, mopping.
Seaweed clings to my heel.
Aching for a chuckle,
I'm the one to fissure out
before the punchline. I'm the one
to sigh for the argyle weave
on a muscular back
that breaststroked away
and away.

When Green Changes Its Mind

Jewel tones rouse me tonight
    the emerald of my dreaming then
        pantina of memory.

Lost in the frisky waltz of willow tree grove
    my Peter Pan felt hat jostled by the wind now
        9-to-5-too-early-to-retire.

Our first kiss atop a mossy tree trunk
    key lime pie of young love and marriage now
        Cigna gaps and stubborn arthritis.

Son's Ninja Turtle garb and horseplay charms
    comic relief for grade-school buddies now
        millennial angst on Facebook.

Ten thousand light years long—ghostly tails
    of glowing green gas light up deep space. How
        a practiced telescope brokers distance.

Blood-Dark

My bed rotates on the tip
    of a fingernail moon.
The compass, a steady south in the attic
    where mice and bats stir worry.
Two a.m. mother to son—
    Where are you tonight?
For days no return calls.
    No Facebook posts.
Silence my heart's cacophony.
    My skin a prickly field.
Are you cloaked, choked
    by the dark debris of your thinking
clot of your blood-dark
    fist holes through drywall?
It seems you've misplaced yourself
    so far from where you started
sulking under seats and
    in overhead compartments.
Consumed by your gravity chores,
    the broom your only tomorrow.
I bend over your cradle to find
    the jagged lists you left behind,
mathematics of your pain,
    scab that is your childhood.
Your core samples lock away,
    memory-ash your repository,
and here I am stranded trying
    to read wavelike drifts of snow.
Like knucklebones, the clock fractures.
    I fill lacuna with another pulled card
from Dali's tarot, frolic of the breeze.

    The hierophant knows you
are the embryo in the lantern,
    seed for the cypress tree,
the bread the wine on the table.
    Numinous wink clarifies,
cleansed of habit's dust.
    It's okay not to be yourself.
Be all yourselves.
    The bullseye can survive in the margin.
And from deep in the ravine,
    the gnome of night-vision camera grunts:
follow me if you dare, back to sleep.

WITH BAITED BREATH

What I Learned from Ambrose Bierce

> *In 1913, at the age of seventy-one, the famous writer saddled up a horse and rode into Mexico. He disappeared without a trace.*
>   Forest Gander, "Very Trustworthy Witnesses,"
>   *The Paris Review*

My story pales, sometimes slapdash,
sometimes elegiac, my stunt double,
wave of ten thousand starlings. But
lately, Ambrose, you've visited my

dreams. You urge me, with your
dual-edged charm and twist endings,
to pick up on context as I trudge
behind you through merciless brush

of Mexico's Zone of Silence. Our
footsteps chime through lacy shadows
that whisper how you will be museumed.
I am a pauper of timid trajectory while

you, with skull in your palm, are celebrity
of your story, speculation has kinged you.
Did you wrap another hoax
around your shoulders or head

south for sombrero and revolution?
Old Gringo, you harvested many
deaths there: boiled alive near a
Mayan temple, gripped by pneumonia

on a two-wheeled cart, submerged in
maelstrom of tequila topped with riddle
of bullets, or evaporated while walking
a well-worn path. O Bitter Bierce,

my stubborn specter is not bloody Shiloh,
Chickamauga, or Kennesaw Mountain,
but simply which day will arrive as my
finale for the heavy paw of obscurity.

Destiny News

for Bob Fox, writer and blues musician (1943-2005)

When someone knocks
on your cranium in a dream
you should open your eyes
and pay them attention.
Like taking a forkful
of a moist slice
of coconut cake after
the server at Denny's
plops it wobbly on the table.
So hello again, Bob,
your moustache dense like
a warm bowl of morning
oatmeal and your breath
burned into the skin
of your CDs. The idea
of your leaving
still tucked away
in my glove box,
the helium
in your tutelage
made us all rise.
You were no
Yiddish journalist but
Meigs County cropper who
detested the stuffiness
of gentleman farmer
and shaped subway
fables even past
the ninth inning.

Now it's elsewhere
stirred by a mystic
dream board—
so hello, middle-
of-the-night visitor.
You're still strongly
in deed, fresh
as the news, traveler
on destiny's meridian.

All the Days of Forgetting

    for Marc

Colors perceived exactly
as they aren't. How do you
prize apart light from paint,
map warm with cool.
In roux of madder red, in
lift-off of dragon's blood
you frame a nub of myth—
rhythms of hush.
In pure breaths of forgetting
we inhale no word, no plot,
no fashion, no tangle,
just portal to dissolve
and vanish into fresh.

Midnight at the Mill

(anonymous artist engraving of historic Lanterman's Mill
in Youngstown, Ohio found during renovation)

Chiaroscuro charmstone,
map of waterfall's light,
echo chamber
gently lifted
from ash and dust.
Blessed be nameless hands
that speak, etch paradigm
through time—
its milky fire
of night sky,
luminous mists,
full moon's canticle
for a grinding house
with manna showers
of buckwheat and corn.

Is that Dante nodding
from deep shadows?
Dore whispering
into the pulse of vigil?
Blessed be a lost engraver
who freeze-framed
alpha and omega—
our Holy Cinematographer's
claim to fame.

The Haserot Angel Holds Court

(Lake View Cemetery; Cleveland, Ohio)

How esctatic the dead must be
having first emerged
from that secret place of
mother immersion to then return
to this hushed belly of lawn.
To drink dusk deeply from gardens
with fireflies, owls, tree frogs,
crickets and delicious slice
                      of moon.

Across a mighty marble
throne, the seated Soul Bird
expands its wings. Breath
swells borderless, speaks
without gender. Black tongues
of tears trail its bronze cheeks,
seep from hollow eyes, patina
grief for Haserot family
                      bones.

From hem of robe, its naked
toe points our way. Should we
offer feathers, blossoms,
pennies, pine cones at its feet?
Do we dare sit on its inevitable
lap, this *Angel of Death Victorious*,
its hands cupped and cradling
a strident torch inverted,
                      extinguished?

Row, Row, Row Your Exquisite Boat

    for composer John Williams

Birthed in darkness and surfacing
from the liminal, how lush your lush
that surges and sways in the movies.

Marvels of your leitmotifs
with balletic textures sailing through—
echoes of old Hollywood romance,
the outflung arms of fanfare,
gossamer friendship in flight against
a luminous full moon.

It's your florid exuberance of polyphony
or your vector of two fearsome notes.
It's your tuba voice of mothership,
your simple syntax blooming in first contact,
your haunting violin that weeps for Holocaust.

Your melodies catch in the trees
and orbit the stars.
You are ear worm charmer
leaving cineplex for whistle or hum.

You are inventive comrade
of screenplay and camera,
working out the ending for us
with agile harmony or tender hymn
launched from Paleolithic breaths
that rolled across the reeds
of holy vibration.

Husk

after the sculpture by Kristen Newell

Let us say after months and months,
slanted and stained, you turn
yourself inside out to travel far
from wanting, you plant your feet
to elongate your stance, you scale
serpentine steps snaking up
your calves, you channel dark
melodies from the mulberry tree
rooted into the cavern of your
belly. Let's say your collar and
chest are dotted with tiny windows
where inside, levels deep, a hive
of galaxies sparked then seared
and you strain to conjure
the synapse of a few sparkling
chapters—Tinkertoy bridges,
sock-monkey playmates, whispers
of your nickname smooth as
jasper skipped across a pond.
Say you nod to the nothing
more than this husk of you
and looking outward, arms
above your shoulders, hands
clasped behind your head,
your hinged face swings
open, final fulcrum,
to release all of us
you will leave behind.

Stepsisters at Large

    for Claude Cahun (1894-1954)
    and Marcel Moore (1892-1972)

Fueled and fused
by enigma and art,
you were one,
you were the other,
Lucy and Suzanne,
more Claude and Marcel,
your lifeblood paired—
truth uncanny
plus rebel muse.

girls>>grok
garnish>>gamble

In cafe culture
you became a couple of foxes
who could display and hide
in simultaneous wonder,
tantalizing bait,
irritating charm,
you made a body speak
in hundreds of ways,
signs within signs,
montages dreaming
more montages,
masquerade as bedrock,
masks with no eyeholes,
arms spidering out
from stone,
human rag doll

tucked into a shelf,
female dandy dandy
in chessboard coat,
stars on cheeks,
nipples on shirts,
heads inside bell jars,

Gildas of trousers,
Sapphos in love.

You were sacrifice,
test of moral argument,
crafted nodal points
of confrontation, subversive
tracts poking out from
barbed-wire fences,
cigarette packets
stuffed in your old lady
pockets, all bets on for
agitating Nazis, prison,
the fait accompli.

reprieve>>retrieve
taboo>>redo

and here we are
in the lobby
of what you left behind,
of what was long lost,
and of what's beside
your timeless,
unnerving,
persistent points.

Dolly Parton, a Theory of

> *Her power is to open what is shut;*
> *shut what is open.*
> —Diane Di Prima

When the rhythms of snapping beans set in,
wildflowers laced her lilting sighs. Vainglorious
Southern-fried double agent—the law
of dynamics set her on her way high-octane
angel with allegiance to the thrill of cartwheel
and *pretty enough to get by*. On dry-cleaner tickets
and gum wrappers, she knew the legacy of
showing her work, the sine and cosine of wigged
latitudes and waists cinched to the nines.
Her pronouns—battery radio, Grand Ole Opry,
and Crossover, too. She is latticed universe, legislator
of the luxury of future, medium for So Much Jangle
and Fringe. She is premise of umbrella sky, beehive
tattoo, and what blooms from constructs of hardscrabble.

Chef-O-Nette

Free-floating and sharp-edged, her whispered wisecracks sashay to the beat of forked and spooned chatter. Deep into desire's penchant for nostalgia, patrons crane over steamy ivory mugs, comet tails of fried shrimp, surreal planets of Jell-O salad. Next to pink tracksuits and frayed polo shirts, her crisp uniform clings close to the bone while she still believes in fishnet and Estée Lauder crimson for launching *SugarPies* and *Sweeties*. In the break room between double shifts, she sips Geritol shots and Nietzsche, dabs anti-wrinkle eye cream, scrawls credit card payments minimum and late. She draws happy faces on Guest Check pads and refuses to stifle—when their eyes won't glance up from their crosswords—a luscious *No Problem*. Two a.m. and a short walk home, milkshake and cold fries for supper, coins and wrinkled bills into the cookie jar, and then prone on her dead mother's Persian hand-knotted wool and silk rug her arthritic fists uncoil, releasing minnows from her palms.

Freeway Ramp

At its end and outside his story,
a human rag of overcoat,
eyes lowered, rusty knuckles
under ragged mittens
that clutch a cardboard totem,
stained with weeping Sharpie
and weary from a litany
of chilled night foldings.
Now in his graveled space,
inverted ash can for resting in the sun,
his body shrunk by nature, corners
of his mouth failing, punctum
of dense cataracts,
Russian roulette of a life.
He is not yet ready to disappear,
divine revelator of what can thrive
bleak but back. Hot coffee,
cheese sandwich, little of what
I can offer some mornings
on my way to work for the precise
condition of his bowed head
nodding with vapor breath.

Dietrich

after The Devil is a Woman (1935)

You are trickster moon ready for your close-up
dangling to ensnare, caress, distress the boys
the men who light watchfires for you
your lacquered lips suckling satellite cigarettes.

Sultry coyote who slinks predatory
in the ways of Berlin.
You will pin them with your eyes,
lashes (fringed parasols)
eyebrows (arched arrows)
emerging again and again from jungles
of atmosphere the conceal, the reveal,
passion for artifice.

Honey-coated tongue and trousers
for clandestine sewing circles
box-office playbook puppetmaster
in every slight, seductive turn of kaleidoscope.

Whiskey tenor, champagne effervescence
halo of Shalimar and clove
so much clinging satin,
so many exotic pearls, veils, furs,
feathers framed by calculus of desire
while maternal seams fray.

Slender queen of hearts,
erotic tilt-a-whirl who
knows how to slice
the heavens for sacred key light.

You are melting sugar that renews,
embellishes into gold-studded bonbons
again and again.

Passenger in slim body, ravenous and readied
to harvest ripe peaches of immortality
and the fleeting favor/flavor of ellipses.

KINDRED RECKONING

for Hash Halper, Ellen McIlwaine, and Romulo Yanes
    (all New York Times obituary subjects, July 4, 2021)

His clusters of little chalk hearts drawn on city sidewalks,
a New York romantic walking barefoot in Soho
    the magic of
    topped with a dollop of
    from every corner of
    a street artist's zigzag of
    a Brooklyn bridge jump-off of
    last straw of
    in search of

Gutsy white woman once-upon-a-time-half-a-Jimi-Hendrix-
duo, seducing her own slide guitar before he turned fame
    higher ground of
    she big-voice honkytonk angel of
    the in and out of
    way past fifteen minutes of
    but still the product of
    yawing chasm of
    male upper hand of

Prized photographer's lens for pristine melon balls and
string-laced turkeys,
amorist of food, delicious with his eye, sexy blackberry jam
or asparagus spear
    now slick Instagram filters of
    swarms of wannabes of
    foodie loyalists of
    the other end of
    glossy magazine covers of
    art-form pioneer of
    pristine light and layering of

When chalk hearts wash away or cancers worm their way
into noble stories of

What Belongs to the Moment

    after Don Penn's photograph, *The Butoh Dancer*

Stirring stardust particles
                        from the starkness
of abandoned barn with its weary floorboards
                              and the swirling mist
      of double exposure.

      Body empty, deep and wide
            thread of life pulls, unravels,
erupts, recedes. Rhythms inside
                  rhythms. From solar plexus
      mountain trembles, shoulders comb
            the clouds, river slows from eyes.
        Spiders tucked inside palms,
                smoke clings to thighs, arms
infinite branches to snag duende.
            Feet transmute into the underside
of planets. Body an evaporating
              cobweb, a long bag that sways
into the dance of darkness.

What silence can conjure.
      What moment can beckon
            from the void.

How to Outwit Oblivion

> after *Artemisia* (2020 catalogue from The National Gallery in
> London) and for painter Artemisia Gentileschi (1593-1653)

We reread across centuries to retrieve you,
your canvases suspend elastic moments like, and

not like other Baroques. Seconds split open, rhythms
of your tread. By stuttering candlelight you are lungs

of your house. Your zaftig women whispering *God
Oh God*, their horror/their ligaments of desire

look right through us. The Russian dolls from your
badger-hair brush—women within women, echoed

currency of your face, grammar of their manly
hands. You, eager girl protégé who took bites of

raw sunrise, a caged goldfinch in your father's
bottega. Hungry eyes, you learned to think with

your body, muscle of your lens, beetroot on your lips,
dark undercoat and Gentileschi golds for suffering

heroines. Time slips. Rape trial in tabloid moon shadow.
Dissertations, movies, novels torque your story, wedge

you into what's illustrative. You, royal artist for parceled
flesh tones and calibrated scenes. You, maestra who finds

purchase again and again. Seemed seams of history
intervene, and you standing on top of the stars,

your signature in Clio's open book,
your ear-finger wagging.

Resurrection Letter: Leonora, Her Tarot, and Me (in Seventeen Parts)

> *Even though you won't believe me,*
> *my story is beautiful*
> *And the serpent that sang it*
> *Sang it from out of the well.*
>   Leonora Carrington, 1917-2011

You birthed your own, deep-rooted tarot from the penumbra.
First, your Fool, leader of the suite
and his fist of a deck that he bibles with occult
tchotchkes. He's counting on me
to be a hot read looking to rearrange
myself, to rub my face away
like a clown teetering
in the ghost light, to avoid the gangplank
that's splotched with quick sand.
I listen for his red wand's hum
and swish of feather duster that I may enter
the Wonder Tent having hung a deer skull
from my apartment window
in hopes that my name will be writ
in sugar and that
the handle of my mother's porcelain teacup
from which I sip her Swee-Touch-Nee
will be shaped
like an angel.

[beginnings]
You were born for that gooey nougat center with
refusal to pay any gravity bills, leaping continents
as if they were stepping stones. At dawn you were
wakened by peonies exploding beneath your
bedroom windows, fat black ants soldiering off
in lines of duty to carry you off to sea. You relished
breakfasts of black-olive puppets on your fingertips,
played with Chinese bric-a-brac in your mother's sitting
room, fancied chocolates rolling around in your cheeks.
You birthed fantastic creatures in your journals and liked
calling out for beings hiding in their underworlds. You fled
stuffy classrooms by closing your eyes for levitation and
heeded your allergies to local gentry and cheery polish.
You knew you were destined for worlds built on clouds,
never to be shoe-horned or conjured or debutanted.
You assassinated every prim nickname and
championed toothy hyenas in high heels, your
faithful understudies in ball gowns or prom dresses.

[genesis]
To this day, you and I can't stop thinking of that Apple, Apple
that stayed for months to teach us how to draw blood
from any circumstance and not be afraid to let our seams
show. We earned every color we applied. Don't make us
take off our earrings we warned any muzzy soul that
pawed at our door. But we were equal parts omission and
inclusion and we craved what could hold us to the path,
what could keep our days and nights furred. Yes,
we were scowling young women in trousers reading
Les Enfants Terrible which reminds us now that we
were simultaneously beauty and beast, raked and raking,
ready to recast a narrow, stubborn world.

Pick a card any card, you are Magician,
a Trickster with shape-shifter countenance.
Hermetic instruments pose on your table.
Infinity plays havoc. Your sly hat, your first card,
your continuous card of occult notions
that encode your trailhead, a sister moon
who whisks alchemy stew in her cauldron,
eerie interiors of your spaces, your painted toys of it,
your gaze now infused, your compass needle
unfurls us both into sequined tunnels.

[lovers]
Our mothers, poems with three engorged teats, delicious
morbidities. Pheasant feathers restless in our ears,
our furniture dreams of hot-house caprice. We nuzzled
with artist lovers under quilts of black cherries, our manes
spreading like Rorschach tests because we had been two
children never threatened by nightingales. There was no
winning us around by gothic mansions, candlesticks in
paternal fists, who preferred cracking hazelnuts between
their toes. We were French lingerie and steeped Earl Grey.
We were thigh-high red boots and tapioca with squid ink.
We were spleens of desire and wayward breezes of
of present tense. We were magical first meetings:
Max of champagne, Gus of Boone's Farm. We pledged
allegiance to rocking horses in our nurseries, pink
Schwinns in hairpin turns. Before we left, we released
every bird from our dovecotes then snatched our suitcases
packed to the gills with clotted vine. Our delinquent
pleasures.

The Hermit, in his shaman's cloak
of red downy feathers and mermaid tail,
points the way with toe in a striped yellow sock.
Destination, a womb that's a small farmhouse
in rural France where his lantern
will give glow to sphinx and mermaid,
vigilant guardians clinging to walls in deep joy.
Portal with art on ceilings. Art in all crevices.
Sun and moon honeyed each day.
Art in every exhale and inhale.
Canvases and canvases of you painting him,
he painting you.
The flame, the heat, then frigid light.
A Hitler, a War,
your mind clouded by sharp objects
thus the Nine of Swords
pulls from the deck.

[sanitarium]
Incessant itching blooms from fire
within—committed for everyone else's good.
Climbing out from a car's womb, you walk sideways
like a crab and light another Marlboro. It is frigid.
Bleating sheep perish all around you. You are bell jar.
You are fenced rebellion. You are Spanish olive brine.
Your identities refract. Map approaches, mock-solemn and
you are down under, your voluptuous thighs beckon.
You are a high-wire performer, straight-jacketed
in magic circle, shrill creature lush with lore but deemed
dangerous with knife and fork by brute structures who try
to glue you together. Your brakes are jammed, you are strapped
naked in your bed, sparks arc unreliable and elusive,
yet you know how to read secret telegrams of vibration.
You descend, needle absessing your thighs, needle again,
again. Your narrating selves arrive in remnants.
In the orchard you walk with walking sticks
of philosophy. Wasn't that sky? The vast swath of it,
the tepid fringes of your sanity scrapbook.
You resurface, the map's M not Madrid but Me.
You arrange your cosmic objects: Tabu powder,
night cream, nail buff boat. Stability an invention
in a liquefied world yet on the tip of your tongue.
Wallpaper's revelation, casserole on your doorstep,
triangles explain everything.

The hour approaches. Luna moth
calls on me, calls me out.
Moon card drawn.
Between gateway of twin towers,
the waxing and waning of your Moon journey.
Sunlight lends its shadows, feeble meadow lends its ground.
Moonlight straddles our path as we walk arm in arm
with our companions, Chance and Divination.
Your cards, your hermetic handbook.
Dog and wolf howl upwards, crayfish climbs
towards your faceless orb whose droplets of light
water its good omen—
in order to be,
go where you are not.

[escape]
You and I flee from hometowns of too many haircuts,
too many slices of white bread, too much cheap beer
guzzled in Speedway parking lots. You flee to tightly
packed alleyways and terracotta rooftops of Lisbon
for WWII refugees and secret agents, the stuff of
Casablanca and *Casino Royale*. Urgent need for gloves
can get you there through the back door of a cafe
and into wedlocked arms of a Mexican Embassy.
My urgent need for ass on the back of a bad boy's
Harley. Your passport to America with generous husband
of convenience, tentacles of Hitler and Lord Candlestick
can't reach across Atlantic. Emma's visceral Statue,
hotbed of surrealism in Manhattan's forest of skyscrapers,
all artists in exile. Our canvas no longer big enough.
Hot plate and ramen noodles in revolving motel rooms.
Alchemy kitchen of sixteenth century, hares stuffed with oysters,
restaurant mustard slathered on your feet. Horse reborn,
mud lark poised. We both finally turn our backs
on the bird superior and leap.

Five is middle. We are in between
two worlds. Material behind us,
spiritual ahead.
In black cloak we are uncertain
but bridge is offered
across river
and of five cups,
two still stand.

[hearth]
We do pilates on the ceiling, our heads jump along
behind us. Teams of cats nuzzle spine by spine on quilts.
We swing our new sons in circles, marvel at tiny toes, tend
to their boo-boos, freeze their grins in snaps. Geranium and
peony. Everything growing and aglow. Baby daddies know
how to tickle bloody well. We are mother goddesses, halo of wheat,
in our palms little furry eggs, open-mouthed. Our house of loving
opposites—art studio atop a carport, subterranean writing desk
in Tiki room, all brimming with milk of our dreams.

Navigating through muted domain,
what can be affirmed; what can be denied.
You pull from your imaginal affair The Chariot,
balance of all we need under a canopied tent,
two hybrid sphinx and harpy with a shared blue heart—
today, no 8 of Cups can deflate me.

[conduit]
Art our vehicle of transport where we archive
and curate all we encounter with oil or ink or pulse.
Dreams saturate us, dreams within dreams strange
only to strangers. We make maps of a million interiors
for our inner populations, the borders for liminal space
blade thin. Anima and animus deep in our pockets.
Shadow's panorama in fluid vortex. Laconic tales
flicker and transform. She-beasts hold their heads
high, so many Bosch concoctions, celestial
to terrestrial with immense silences in midair.
Our gaze is frontal in duel with our viewers
whom we want to come to life as if they'd always
been there. Our intoxicating task, bones
of our being, cups of our tea.

You are Priestess who writes backwards
and while they're sleeping, you may snip
a lock from their hair
to stir into their morning's omelette.
Your wolf tooth gladly marries
gold and silver leaf.

[laboratory]
In our homes of Sphinx, chaos our mentor,
detritus our picnic. Children's toys, cooking utensils,
books and books and books and artist tools strewn,
nothing enslaved by housekeeping. Egg tempura
brews with eggs Benedict—we are guardians
of the Egg of the World. We distill and transform,
we stir the cauldron, birds fly from our cloaks,
cabbage our rose. Kitchen (tabernacle's oxygen
of magic) where rules crack open and potions
summon our drive, our pilgrim's path.

Tonight The Fool and The Hanged Man
arrive together.
Cards pressed back to back.
Hair dives downward,
invisible hands clutch amulets.
From living wood scaffolding,
legs suspend in dancerly pose
in a place all lavender and gold.
Power of inverted elevation
offers me spiritual pause
to mark threshold.
A fool's modest knapsack
over my shoulder,
forward I stretch
on the way to you.

[finale]
Maiden/mother/crone—roiling in the labyrinth
with three heads. We grey and wrinkle and age spot.
We grasp spectacles, hearing trumpets, glasses
of port. Face app shows me my ninety-four. Coffee table
tome shows me yours. Facebook hisses
and preens. Less time for quick cuts, I'm now
on the train of slow pans that I watch through
gaps of my fingers. You continue hardcore and
fluid. Me, I don't know what to do
with myself alone in my furnished stable.
Pomegranate jewels bleed into my palms.
I shun thimbles, prefer corners to hide in.
You forever Leonora, wild and tender,
river-wide, endurance warrior, modern novel
with eyes of black stars, horse shadow.
Leonora, Leonora, of course, of course.
I surrender this letter to you.

END TRAILS

Hand Shadows

Stubby, curled digits
thrill in childhood memory
of flashlight under bedsheets
for wagging tails, wiggling
bunnies and waving birds
in flight, matters of ideas
thrown upon the wall.

A woman blows out a candle.
She pulls a blanket to her chin,
exhales a Marlboro before
twisting its butt into a bedside saucer.
She closes her eyes and rehearses
tomorrow. She drifts off. Shadows
stripe her fingers. Moonlight
drinks her in.

A man thumbs the slide switch
of a flashlight in the red glow
of his car's dashboard.
His leather gloves, raven black.
He strokes the eyeball trinket
on his key ring, and parks
down the street.

A woman sets another match
to a candle wick. Her bedroom
fragrant as a garden
in cool moonlight.
A man wears leather gloves,
raven black, turns key
in a back door lock,

tiptoes toward a bedroom.
A woman grips the butt
of a handgun from
a nightstand drawer,
its shadow a cobra on the wall.
The moon waits outside
in a cloudless sky
silent, gleaming, sure.

Release Recurring

> after Céline Sciamma's *Portrait of a Lady on Fire*

Amniotic churning of rough sea, the painter reinvents herself. Scaling pelvic bone of cliff, instinct will harness her hunger to be twinned. In an eighteenth-century chateau immense quiet is alert to isolate each rustle of petticoat, shivering tongues of candle or fireplace, scratches from charcoal on tight canvases of uncalcined umber. Eyes of the painter and her muse agree in the craft of craving capture, rapture of their mouths sends paper lanterns to the moon, pubis cradles self-portrait, perfect skin luminous, beholder becomes beheld, beheld becomes beholder. Legend maroons them on this remote shore where time and timelessness intersect. Their gazes for each other fixed in tableaus. Color bars of Vivaldi, what another Orpheus chooses, wedding dress apparition portends. A woman's world takes charge—a cappella canticle with witchy bonfire, hem catches flame. With cedar root, pennyroyal and skewer, a young housekeeper brings down the flowers of pregnancy and painter takes her place as rare recorder. Art always seeks its fulcrum between liberation and captivity. Muse finally released to canvas.

> Lovers released from patriarchy to the salve of recurring recollection deep in their bones.

> Muse finally released to canvas because Art always seeks its fulcrum between liberation and captivity. Young housekeeper brings down the flowers of pregnancy with cedar root, pennyroyal, and skewer, while the painter takes her place as rare recorder. Hem catches flame. A cappella canticle with witchy bonfire. A woman's world takes charge. Color bars of Vivaldi, what another Orpheus chooses. Wedding dress apparition

portends. Their gazes for each other fixed in tableaus where time and timelessness intersect. Legend maroons them on a remote shore. Beholder becomes beheld, beheld becomes beholder. Perfect skin luminous, pubis cradles self-portrait. Rapture of their mouths sends paper lanterns to the moon. Eyes of the painter and her muse agree in the craft of craving capture. Scratches from charcoal on tight canvases of umber. Shivering tongues of candles and fireplaces, rustle of petticoats. The immense quiet alert to isolate in an eighteenth-century chateau. Instinct harnessing the hunger to be twined, she scaled pelvic bones of cliff. The painter reinvented herself. Amniotic churning of rough sea.

Blood

for Ma'Khia, 4/20/21

A man ahead of me in the grocery checkout
can't stop praising chainsaws—their visceral
growls drilling deep into his woods snarling
dominance. In his cart, a stack of cellophaned
flesh and muscle. *Bloody steak is what I crave*
he pronounces and I choose to lower my eyes
and not enlighten him that what he thinks is
blood oozing onto his dinner plate is just water
braided with myoglobin. I imagine he could be
hosting suckers and hooks in darkish start for
a Mobius strip of tapeworm, its solitary
confinement, his gut. Hitchcock's shower scene
sent chocolate syrup down the drain. My friend,
whose Halloween home could be a movie set,
showcases his recipe of corn syrup, red food
coloring, and cocoa mix.
So the blood is not the blood, except for all
the recent mass shootings and today when
a frenzied teenage girl in my hometown, shot
dead by police, is freeze-framed on a driveway
beneath a car door when the unfurled syntax
of her rainbow clogs and a steak knife delivers
the coiled underbelly of foster-care-broken,
her life seeping into pavement, while a jury
presents their guilty verdict for another
killing, this time at the knee of an officer
and I imagine these Twilight Zone episodes
we're consuming almost daily are flatworms
deep within us, eggs hatching, infection
surging, our systems growing numb.

Golden Shovel: She Just Packed up Her Stuff and Left*

for Marie Petry Heiser

Finally, with pointillistic sensitivity, a DNA
reading has added to the incomplete profile
of your life, what the house of your body still tells. Mandala of mystery identifies
you now. Candle, rock garden, flower arrangement, all that remains
as tribute to how you took in the world as
toddler, school girl, wife, then mother
whose son and daughter were told by their father that you packed up your stuff and left. Yet, who
was the murderer who deposited your nakedness in a ditch, fingered your last pulse, just
more tragedy that if a survellience camera had been there, it could have packed
up the truth. Today, detectives try to harvest what a genealogy tree stirred up,
quivering petals in the current. For forty years you were a nameless her
with souvenirs fading, blonde strands in the teeth of your hairbrush, stuff
that children hold close like the tender coaxing of tiny fingers into mittens and
a flimsy veil that your sudden leaving, without causality or agency, left.

* *DNA Profile Identifies Remains as Mother Who 'Just Packed Up Her Stuff and Left' by Michael Levenson; The New York Times*, March 28, 2021

Box Like No Other

after Bruno Casiano's painting Television

You're so last century. In polished wood cabinetry, you appeared in living rooms for sound + sight in even bigger furniture consoles than radio. Remember Checkers speech. Remember moon landing. Remember *to the moon, Alice, to the moon*. All the kids in my neighborhood whined to be at the feet of our family TV, first color set on the block. On Saturdays my brother and I pulled drapes tight and dipped buttery Lorna Doone bites into milk mugs along with tasty high jinx from *The Flintstones*, *Space Ghost*, and *Cool McCool*. Praise chewing gum for our eyes. Praise fizz and pop, tight and fast. Praise remote switching better than sex. McLuhan was probably right—images wrap around us because we are the screen and vanishing point for ogle and gape in the politics of gaze. Lure us to crave classier kitchens that dangle erotic cuisine. Deliver us to the handling in laugh track and sound bite. Take us live to war zones and mass shootings for soggy thoughts and prayers. Underthought continues to elude us as Box evolves into mega screen culture. Swift versions with surround sound and galaxies of pixels now carry us onto the far reaches of a still needful planet.

The Alchemy of View

My windows speak for December's calligraphy
of the Japanese maple my father planted for first
grandchild or they invite gentle reasoning of
breeze that sips the perfume from my mother's
lilacs frothy each spring. My windows enter my
home with companions of sun or moon to seduce
jazzy bedroom wallpaper or animate endearing
clutter atop heirloom furniture and in kitchen sink.
Our eyes won't hesitate to lend meaning to our
meaning—narrow and dense as a beam traveling
from lighthouse, how a chipped teacup once held
the warmth of her hot-spiced gin.

Some Security Questions

What was the month/day/year when your mother took back her maiden name after the bastard left? What is your go-to weapon of resistance when you're not given a drop-down menu? How many memory wanks did you experience last night in the shower? How many times did your parents cheat on the gender predictor quiz when you were in utero? When did your birthday learn to take U-turns? Who is your favorite friend who knows less than they think they know? How many times did your preference for black licorice gumdrops seem fixed until your new lover fed you pitted black olive puppets from her fingertips? Which cuss word does your Skyrim avatar demand that you tattoo onto your forehead? What is your tracking number for prayers? How many of your Shih Tzus have you had frozen in a cyronic state? Where in Las Vegas do you usually meet up with your fears? What is your guardian angel's CB radio handle? How many you's can prove that you really are you?

Ode to the Candidate Commercials of Ohio's Special 15th Congressional Seat Election August 2021

O endorsement battles of sphincter jowls,
    deceit snaking across thy foreheads.
Thy receding piers of attention span,
    thy liver-spotted handshakes.
Bloody sonnets of rifle scopes in glory iambic pentameter.
    Blest No-Mask, No-Vax, all steel-toed for righteous
body freedom. Still thou art two-faced, closed-eyed robbers
    of female body rights for breeding.
O excuses carbonated. O policies brutish.
    Thou strive to nick the jugular of any leading
Other as we the people cling to wobbly rafts
    with splintered, rotting rudders.

Yard Signs for the Apocalypse

In This House We Believe In
ironic paraphernalia
jumbled typefaces
blogs that pant and drool
speaking with the manager

In This House We Believe In
pink-crocheted beanies
scrapbooks of static
the latent philosophy of tater tots
Bundt cakes that know how to testify

In This House We Believe In
pinball tunes of washer/dryer combos
Chihuahuas that wear lipstick
futures that refuse their present
therapists who prescribe cages in cages

In This House We Believe In
waters we've stepped in
the salt and pepper of the masses
the morbid quintain
and of course, sanctimonious final lines.

Tipping Points

If you like ghost punches, AR-15s, and vanishing
    doomsday hitchhikers, then you will like
    graveyards growling with cats
    and accordion facts posing
    like contortionists.

If you like conspiracy theories that sprout
    chin hairs overnight, then you will like
    Sunday revival meetings that sugar
    flapdoodles and firewalkers armed
    with floating-rubber-duckie fortitude.

If you are malcontent with globalists who refuse
    to see what's flat, then you will like
    snapdragon puppetry with fringe
    fringing fringe that pitches
    and rolls against the lighthouse
    in the woods.

If you think moon landings have marinated
    too long in subterfuge, then you will like
    a frayed Abbey Road album cover
    with a *Paul is Dead* T-shirt tucked
    inside its cardboard sleeve.

If tin foil is your haberdashery and hive reasoning
    your Karaoke, then you will like
    sort of's to punctuate your circles
    circling circles to the rhythm
    of freeze—wait—reanimate.

If you like your arguments sipped with
    burnt morning decaf, then you will like
    keeping your grade-school valentines
    in your freezer right behind
    a Spam casserole and a bag
    of psilocybin mushrooms.

If you think he will be definitely coming and you're thinking
    of ways to unroof your home, then you will like
    the friendly brethren who park
    their racing-striped
    turbo saucers
    behind Walmart's
    loading dock.

If you think a shopping list you jotted down
    in the middle of the night came through
    a vibratory frequency, then you will like
    moisturizing with WD-40
    you'll be purchasing today
    along with jumper cables
    commercial-grade.

If you find yourself ripping off metal zippers
    from your trousers and brass eyelets
    from your shoes, then you're rock-ribbed
    and ready to be dipped
    in stardust
    by the scruff.

The Expectation of More
(A Golden Shovel after Shakespeare)

How to find happiness when our default is to
always seek more, to be
collectors of shiny geegaws or
selfies crowding our phones—satisfaction yes yet evanescent, not
the quiet and simple wonders that are there to
tame us with their indifference, but we persist to be
laden with lives baroque, so much stuff that
frays the present tense into flimsy and it is
only when we tilt our heads up to the
evening sky that we temper the involute question.

What's Left on the Plate

See the moon? It hates us.
    Donald Barthelme

We are low-watt bulbs dangling and disordered
    discounting the skies with our hungry tycoons
who lust after zero gravity through their gift-wrapped
    launches that trail space junk behind them.

We are oceans of soup-like swirls filled with plastic
    flotsam or glaciers that can't hold on any longer.
We remain captivated by atlas of backyard, cursed by diminishing
    lives of creatures wide-eyed in rain forests and savannas.

We are stuck in our orbital lanes whining on TikTok
    or cable TV, reasoning through conspiratorial barks
and huddled head-to-head below cornices of appetite and pride.
    We burrow into the faint history of reading, the squall
of internet, so many magnets for our attention, dangerous
    nonsense we don't know what we're tracking, our
mouths half shut ready to descend just around the bend
    onto whatever will be left on the plate, like a few
shedded zebra lashes.

In Gratitude

Thank you to all the generous editors of journals that believed in my poems and shepherded them into the world. My deep gratitude to the following poets who gift me with friendship and feedback, always knowing just when to push and just when to pull: Steve Abbott, Sayuri Ayers, James Borders, Kathleen Burgess, Sandra Feen, Linda Fuller-Smith, Jennifer Hambrick, Rebe Huntman, Chris Minton, Susann Moeller, Susan Olson, Louise Robertson, Mikelle Hickman-Romine, Chuck Salmons, Anna Soter, and all the good folks from Salon and the Youngstown Poetry Intensive group. I am indebted to Emily Rose Cole, Allison Pitinii Davis, and Barbara Sabol for the grace of their time and attention and for the artistry of their words to frame the energy of this collection, and dear friend Sandra Feen whose poignant photograph graces the cover. And of course, thank you Eric Muhr and the entire Fernwood Press team for rendering this collection with such artfulnesss and integrity. It's an honor to have it take its place in the Fernwood family.

Acknowledgments

Arc Magazine: "Shopping Center Tipsy"
Bear Paw Journal: "Box Like No Other"
Blood & Bourbon: "Chef-O-Nette"
Borrowed Solace Journal: "Missed the Weather Report"
Burningword Literary Journal: "Yard Signs for the Apocalypse"
Connecticut River Review: "How to Outwit Oblivion"
Cool Rock Repository: "Bat Faith"
Creosote: "Alchemy of View"
Ethel: "If You Have To Ask"
Evening Street Review: "Ode to Candidate Campaigns for Ohio's Special 15th Congressional Seat Election, August 3, 2021"
Feral: A Journal of Poetry and Art: "Evergreen"
Glacial Hills Review: "Does Cloud Make You Think of Data or Sky?"
Hotazel Review: "Destiny News"
In Parentheses: "Dining with Parents," "Kindred Reckoning," "When Green Changes It Mind," "Eco Dysphagia"
I-70: "Knots: A Ledger"
Jet Fuel: "Eel Love"
KAIROS Literary Magazine : "On Candy Lane"

Land Luck Review: "Attic"
long con magazine: "Husk"
Main Street Rag: "City Pool Swimming Lesson"
Midwest Zen: "Sijo At Dusk"
Orchard Poetry Journal: "Hand Shadows"
Pinhole Poetry: "Zebra Lashes"
Poor Yorick : "Midnight at the Mill"
Rabbit: "Golden Shovel: She Just Packed Up Her Stuff and Left*"
Remington Review: "Dietrich"
Rough Cut Press: "Tipping Points"
Salt Weekly: "Score for Teapot Duet," "Sleep Study," "What's Left on the Plate"
Sheila-Na-Gig: "Life Poodle," "Some Security Questions," "Some Things I Encountered While Conversing," "Thought, Song"
Slipstream: "Blood-dark," "When Auntie Kissed a Beat"
Snapdragon: "Postcard From Elsewhere)
Steam Ticket: "Chicken Envy," "Food for Thought at Philosophy Hall"
Stone Poetry Journal: "Leavings," "Some Fun Facts About Berries"
The Heartland Review: "Tracy Decay"
The Imagist: "This Autumn My Son"
The Kieksograph: "All the Days of Forgetting," "Stepsisters At Large," "Release Recurring"
The McNeese Review: "Dolly, A Theory Of"
The Museum of Americana: "What I Learned From Ambrose"
The Ocotillo Review: "What Belongs to the Moment"
The Quarter(ly): "Sock," "Manifesto for My Pockets"
The Salt Weekly: "What's Left on the Plate," "Sleep Study," "Score for Teapot Duet"
Trajectory: "The Expectation of More"
Triggerfish: "Blood"
Visions International: "The Haserot Angel Holds Court"
Westerly Magazine: "House of Bears"

"Thought, Song" appeared in the poetry anthology *Birds of the Cuyahoga* published by the Edith Chase Symposium in 2022.

"Evergreen" appeared in the poetry anthology, *Songs for Wild Ohio* published by the Edith Chase Symposium in 2023.

"Resurrection Letter" was published as an illustrated arts chapbook by Cereal Box Studio (2023).

"House of Bears" won a 2022 Winners' Circle Award from the National Federation of State Poetry Societies.

"Dolly Parton: A Theory Of" won first prize in Ohio Poetry Day Association's Special Award in their 2022 poem competition.

"Row, Row, Row Your Exquisite Boat" was featured in a concert by the Youngstown Area Community Concert Band in celebration of film score composer John Williams (2023).

"The Haserot Angel Holds Court' was published in the anthology, *Poem for Cleveland* published by Red Giant Books and edited by Poet Laureate Ray McNiece.

Title Index

A

All the Days of Forgetting 66
Attic 50

B

Bat Faith 15
Blood 104
Blood-Dark 58
Box Like No Other 106

C

Chef-O-Nette 74
Chicken Envy 20
City Pool Swimming Lesson 41

D

Destiny News 64
Dietrich 76
Dining with Parents 49
Does Cloud Make You Think of Data or Sky? 36
Dolly Parton, a Theory of 73

E

Eco Dysphagia 22
Eel Love 17
Evergreen 43

F

Food for Thought at Philosophy Hall 29
Freeway Ramp 75

G

Golden Shovel: She Just Packed
   up Her Stuff and Left 105

H

Hand Shadows 100
House of Bears 13
How to Outwit Oblivion 81
Husk 70

I

If You Have to Ask 26

K

Kindred Reckoning 78
Knots: A Ledger 38

L

Leavings 52
Life Poodle 21

M

Manifesto for My Pockets 30
Midnight at the Mill 67
Missed the Weather Report 53
Morning Collage 35

O

Ode to the Candidate Commercials of
   Ohio's Special 15th Congressional Seat
   Election August 2021 109
On Candy Lane 39

P

Postcard From Elsewhere 34

R

Release Recurring 102
Resurrection Letter: Leonora,
   Her Tarot, and Me (in seventeen parts) 82
Row, Row, Row Your Exquisite Boat 69

S

Score for Teapot Duet 31
Shopping Center Tipsy 46
Sijo At Dusk 19
Sleep Study 32
Sock 56
Some Fun Facts about Berries 48
Some Security Questions 108
Some Things I Encountered While Conversing 27
Stepsisters at Large 71

T

The Alchemy of View 107
The Expectation of More
   (A Golden Shovel after Shakespeare) 113
The Haserot Angel Holds Court 68
This Autumn My Son 51
Thought, Song, ... 23
Tipping Points 111
Trace Decay 54

W

What Belongs to the Moment 80
What I Learned from Ambrose Bierce 62
What's Left on the Plate 114
When Auntie Kissed a Beat, ... 44
When Green Changes Its Mind 57

Y

Yard Signs for the Apocalypse 110

Z

Zebra Lashes 12

First Line Index

A

A man ahead of me in the grocery checkout 104
Amniotic churning of rough sea,
  the painter reinvents herself 102
At its end and outside his story 75

B

Birthed in darkness and surfacing 69

C

Chiaroscuro charmstone 67
Colors perceived exactly 66

E

Every click, tap, and swipe turns 36

F

Father liked to warn me about 12
Finally, with pointillistic sensitivity, a DNA 105
Free-floating and sharp-edged,
  her whispered wisecracks 74

From a camera drone, the running 13
Fueled and fused 71

H

Here we are, a bedazzled crew of yahoos,
    careening in the last 34
Her wobbly handwriting in signature purple ink 52
Hey, Tequila Mockingbird, there's a sparrow's 46
His clusters of little chalk hearts
    drawn on city sidewalks 78
How esctatic the dead must be 68
How to find happiness when our default is to 113

I

I can't decide if my Honey is berry 48
If you have to ask twice what's
    under the hood, you already 26
If you like ghost punches, AR-15s, and vanishing 111
In This House We Believe In 110
It was a brisk, fall evening on campus
    when I had misread the 29
It was my Atlantic 41
I was raised by a Canadian hemlock, her perfume 43

J

Jewel tones rouse me tonight 57

L

Let us say after months and months 70
Lifeblood of curlicues, shlup shlup of
    tongue and snout that 21

M

Meet a willing teapot 31
My bed rotates on the tip 58
My father saw surprises 53

My scribbled life 39
My slippers shuffle me 54
My story pales, sometimes slapdash 62
My windows speak for December's calligraphy 107

N

Noble buck at corn feeder. Broken antler,
    back leg dangling 19

O

O endorsement battles of sphincter jowls 109
One electrode would have been one
    too many but now I have 32
One lasso for landing another
    one-night stand, tightening 38

P

particle, wave, the glorious inhale 23

S

Some say dryers eat us 56
Stirring stardust particles 80
Stubby, curled digits 100

T

The precinct of my night's mind 50
the this / the that / the these / a day 30
This poem passes through wheels of color 35
Thought balloons 27

U

urban stew swizzled her tongue 44

W

We are low-watt bulbs dangling and disordered 114
We're not upside down 15
We reread across centuries to retrieve you 81
We were sugar packet missiles 49

What was the month/day/year
  when your mother took back 108
When someone knocks 64
When the rhythms of snapping beans set in 73

Y

You are a walking flower 20
You are trickster moon ready for your close-up 76
You birthed your own,
  deep-rooted tarot from the penumbra 82
You bring 17
You're so last century.
  In polished wood cabinetry, you 106
Your ginger beard 51
Your swallow bird corpse 22